James Payn

The soldier, the Battle, and the Victory

James Payn

The soldier, the Battle, and the Victory

ISBN/EAN: 9783744759915

Printed in Europe, USA, Canada, Australia, Japan

Cover: Foto ©ninafisch / pixelio.de

More available books at **www.hansebooks.com**

The Soldier, the Battle,

AND

The Victory.

BEING A BRIEF ACCOUNT OF THE WORK OF REV. JOHN RANKIN
IN THE ANTI-SLAVERY CAUSE.

By the Author of Life and Writings of Samuel Crothers, Etc.

CINCINNATI:
WESTERN TRACT AND BOOK SOCIETY.
176 *ELM STREET.*

CONTENTS.

CHAPTER I.
THE PREPARATION.. PAGE 5

CHAPTER II.
GIRDING ON HIS ARMOR.. 17

CHAPTER III.
THE BATTLE... 34

CHAPTER IV.
INCIDENTS ON THE BATTLE-FIELD............................... 95

CHAPTER V.
THE VICTORY...113

CHAPTER I.

THE PREPARATION.

THE world is a battle-field! There is not a single continent—no, not even an island, where the battle between evil and good, sin and holiness, oppression and justice, right and wrong, is not being continually waged. With the Bible in our hands we are not without a knowledge of the reasons of this fact. Many ancient heathen philosophers noticed this fact and were puzzled by it; they knew no way of accounting for it, only by the supposition that there was a good and an evil spirit of equal power in the universe: the one laboring to accomplish good, the other to increase the evil.

Discarding their theory of equal power, their supposition was not so far from the fact in the case. There is an evil spirit, a personal being at work in the world. He is called in the Scriptures, "the Prince of the power of the air," and said "to work in the children of disobedience." He will only be permitted, however, to work for a while. God's plan is to destroy the work of the Devil by the man Christ Jesus—the God-man, Immanuel—and by means of his Church to make known to principalities and powers in heavenly places his manifold wisdom. Eph. iii. 10. This glorious work is in progress, and measured by our short lives it progresses slow, but measured by eternal years it moves onward with rapidity.

To our divine wisdom, indeed, it sometimes appears to move backward, as for example in the massacre of the Huguenots in France, the persecution of our Puritan Fathers in England which finally led to their deserting the kingdom; the Stuarts' "harrying" of the Covenanters in Scotland, and the late effort in our own land to nationalize slavery and then to establish a separate nation with slavery as its corner-stone; but to the eye of Omniscience these were only the results of the inner wheels moving round the great purposes of God; and often after long and patient waiting his people are permitted to see the wondrous working of his hand.

Nor does he always use the instrumentalities which men would select to accomplish his purposes; the soldiers which he employs to fight his battles are not often the mighty, the noble, or the rich, but as it is expressed by an Apostle: "God hath chosen the foolish things of the world to confound the wise;" and "the weak things of the world to confound the mighty," and for securing the end "that no flesh should glory save in his presence. It was therefore in exact accordance with this principle and in the line of God's plan of working to choose the subject of our narrative, and to prepare him for the work which he afterward accomplished.

JOHN RANKIN did not descend from the loins of earthly kings, princes or millionaires, but, what was far better, from those who though untitled, and poor in this world's goods, were nevertheless rich in faith and heirs of the kingdom. His grandfather was brought from Ireland when three years old, and was brought up near Carlisle, Pa., previous to the Revolutionary War. In process of time he married Mary Clendenen; both were of Scotch descent, and members of the Presbyterian Church; and such were their teachings and exemplary walk and conversation that all the members of their numerous family became professors of religion and ardent lovers of their country. Several of their sons, and among them the father of John

Rankin, fought in the war which secured their country's independence. So patriotic was his grandfather and so great was his faith in the triumph of right that he sold his farm for Continental money, which, on account of there being no provision made for redeeming it, afterward became worthless, and he was then reduced to poverty and in consequence of this he emigrated to East Tennessee.

Richard his son, the father of our subject, also afterward removed thither and obtained a thousand acres of land, and amid its almost unbroken wilderness erected a log cabin and a blacksmith shop, which still stand, and where his son Richard, during our late fearful rebellion, lived a loyal man faithful among the faithless.

At that early day (1785) it was difficult to dispose of produce so far from the market, and the interruptions from the Indians were so frequent, that a very scant support was all that Richard Rankin could obtain for his family. He was however a godly man, and though he could not give his children the wealth of the world, he endeavored to point them to the place where true riches is found. Nor did he teach alone by precept as is evident from the fact that summer and winter he was a constant attendant in the house of God, although it was seven miles distant from his residence. No doubt these teachings were well seconded by his wife, who, as well as a long line of ancestors, was a fearer of God, and when she came to die in her eighty-second year, January, 1846, some nineteen years after her husband's death, she found it was no vain thing to serve God, but departed triumphing in her Savior and feeling that the great Shepherd of Israel was with her, lighting and supporting her in the dark valley.

On this forest farm the subject of our

sketch was born, 1793. He possessed a vigorous constitution and consequently in a few years, as was then the custom, he was employed in assisting his mother in her household duties—nursing a younger brother, etc., Soon he was able to assist his father on the farm, and at this work he continued until he was twenty years of age. While thus engaged he had the privilege occasionally of spending a few, and only a few, months at the district school two miles distant. He was thus thrown upon his own resources to obtain an education, and God having implanted in his heart a strong desire to obtain knowledge he spent much of his time, not employed in laboring on the farm, in reading, and writing essays, and in the practice of speaking in which he greatly desired to excel. Thus early was his mind being trained for independent investigation, and the confidence in his own conclusions which enabled him to stand alone in the advocacy of unpopular subjects in days to come was now being obtained.

As early as his seventh year he attended to secret prayer and ardently desired to be a possessor of religion, but for years he neglected to publicly profess his faith and to seek a place among the people of God, and the result was that he was left to doubts and darkness. Only those who follow on to know the Lord have the promise "then shall ye know." Like many young Christians he was troubled about the doctrine of God's sovereignty and predestination—he was afraid to read the ninth chapter of Paul's Epistle to the Romans. He saw the doctrine was there, but he loved it not—this sad event God overruled for good. it is not pleasing to a proud heart.

Years were thus passed in conflict with doubts and fears, relieved however occasionally by glimpses of the sunlight of

God's countenance—sufficient to lead him to connect with the church and to prosecute his education with a view of preaching the gospel. But in this work he had many difficulties to overcome. His father had now a large family and only a very small income, so he could not therefore assist him much in the prosecution of his studies, but it was resolved to make the attempt; accordingly he entered Washington College, East Tennessee, and prosecuted his studies with great diligence, feeling that his first term would be his last. During this period his brother David was killed at the battle of Horse Shoe, a circumstance which threw the whole family into deep distress; but His father obtained the pay and allowance due his son from the Government, and used it in continuing John at college. Before this amount was exhausted, he concluded to obtain a help-mate for him, or in other words a wife who should not

His father obtained the pay and allowance due his son from the Government, and used it in continuing John at college. Before this amount was exhausted, he concluded to obtain a help-meet, or in other words a wife who should not only comfort and encourage him, but do something to provide the means for his education. Such a wife he found in the person of Miss Jane Lowry, a granddaughter of the President of the college.

They were married 2d July, 1814, and, as a result, his parents were relieved from any further expense on his account. We suppose some of our readers will smile at the simple statement so unlike the custom of the present time; he made the shoes which he wore at his marriage, and his wife his wedding coat. The same year he graduated, and under the same efficient President began the study of Theology, reading such books as Boston's

Fourfold State, Harvey's "Theron and Aspasia;" and in due time was licensed by the Presbytery of Abingdon. Among his first efforts at preaching he attempted an extemporaneous discourse, and succeeded as he thought admirably, and concluded he would try again, and thus make preaching easy; but the second time was an entire failure. The Sabbath after this he made the attempt with notes fully written out and the following he gives as his experience: "I got through with the first sermon without difficulty, but in delivering the second one I lost my place in the notes and could not find it again, and was obliged to steer through as I could." I afterward wrote out my discourses in full, and memorized them, and yet this plan did not always save me from difficulty in preaching to the congregations where I was brought up. I had my sermon well memorized and was delivering it with ease when suddenly my memory slipped and my mind lost all its ideas, and my eyes their sight so that I could scarcely see the people. I kept speaking, however, and finally got through, but this circumstance greatly increased my natural diffidence." The result was that he was compelled to study, and thus these failures were overruled by God for making him far more efficient as an expositor of his truth—that truth which when known makes free not only from sin and Satan's power, but also from the oppression of man. His early history had given him self-reliance, and now that he feels the necessity of studying the *word* he is prepared to do it, and God's instrument will be prepared for his work— his soldier for the battles he must fight.

CHAPTER II.

GIRDING ON HIS ARMOR.

IN the fall of 1817, in a two-wheeled carriage drawn by one horse, and with his wife and child, a few articles of furniture, and with seventy dollars in his pocket, might be seen John Rankin, wending his way through Kentucky to the State of Ohio. The reason which led to his change of location was his opposition to slavery. Although he had not yet studied the Scriptures so as to see their clear condemnation of this giant wickedness and its inconsistency with the great law of love, yet his sympathetic nature led him to the conclusion that it could not be right, and he desired to escape from it. The journey from East Tennessee to Ohio was then considered quite an undertaking. It is thus described by the subject of our sketch: " On the morning we left, my father withdrew from the family, without his breakfast, and when we started on our journey he took his horse and rode with us until we entreated him to return home. We then thought that we should meet him no more on earth; it was indeed to us all a deeply sorrowful moment. We pursued our journey over a rough and mountainous road, and our carriage being heavily loaded we could travel but a short distance in a day. In this mountainous wilderness the axletree of our carriage broke in two pieces, and I had to leave my wife and child by the road side, and carry it back some miles to a blacksmith shop to get it repaired." Not willing to travel on the Sabbath, they inquired for a lodging place and finally found one in the house of an infidel who treated them very kindly as far as temporalities were concerned, but he avowed his unbelief in the inspiration of the Scriptures and declared he could not understand the miracle of the loaves and fishes, and therefore would not believe it. During the course of the conversation, however, he avowed that " a Dutchman had cured his toothache by performing some incantations at the root of a tree." He was willing to believe in a miracle performed by a Dutchman, though he could not understand how it was done, but not if performed by the Lord Jesus Christ. Verily infidels are the most credulous of men. The next Sabbath he spent in Lexington, preached, and was helped on his way by kind friends. He next stopped at Paris, and was urged by Rev. John Lyle to turn aside and preach for the congregation of Concord, near that place, which he finally concluded to do until the following spring, there being no slaves in that congregation. His experience as a preacher during this period is thus narrated : " I found it difficult to preach to the same people every Sabbath, and give sufficient variety in my discourses. I was however always careful to select a text that had in it sufficient foundation for a discourse. I never had talent enough to make a sermon out of nothing. While I did not write sermons, I did not cease to make compositions. I discussed with the pen various doctrines of divinity. This I found necessary in order to keep up the habit of thinking clearly, and to enable me to speak with ease and accuracy in the doctrines of the gospel. I had a laborious winter, having the care of a church of over two hundred members, and three places of preaching. The spring came, but in the meantime preacher and people had become attached to each other, and

I concluded to become, at their urgent request, their pastor. The state of the church was rather peculiar. Barton Stone, the founder of the New Light denomination, was pastor of Concord congregation, when he withdrew from the Presbyterian Church. He drew off a large part of the church-members with him, and he continued to propagate his dangerous errors in that neighborhood. He taught that the Father is God, that the Son is the first and greatest Being, begotten and not eternal, not God only as the Father dwells in him; that he died to bear witness to the truth, but made no atonement for sin. He denied the doctrine that God exists in three persons, and he also denied the doctrine of household baptism, and taught that the proper mode of administering it was by immersion. These and other errors I had to meet, with the Bible alone, for as yet I had no library.

"The majority of the people in that section of the State, at that period, were anti-slavery, and though I often spoke and preached against it, I was never molested. During the first year of my ministry, a sick man, some miles distant from my residence, sent for me to visit him. I went at his request, and found him low with consumption. He lived in an ignorant and irreligious neighborhood, and I preached at his house several times through the week, until he died; and although the service was on week-days, there was always a good attendance, and finally the house would not hold the people. After the death of the sick man the preaching was continued in another neighborhood, and finally a congregation was organized, and a house of worship built, and it is believed many in this neighborhood were brought to know, love and serve the Savior. During this period I attended many large religious meetings, at which there was much serious feeling, and many additions made to the churches. One of these revival scenes occurred soon after I became pastor of Concord Church. Rev. John R. Moreland, of Mt. Pleasant, invited me to assist him during a communion season which was continued through several days. The number of people in attendance was so large that no house could hold them, and as a necessity we held the meetings in the open air. While I was preaching on a platform prepared for the purpose, Bro. Moreland became so excited that he suddenly sprung up and clasped his arms around me. This was quite a surprise both to the people and myself; and but for the deep solemnity that pervaded the audience it would have produced mirth. My own feelings were so highly wrought up by the subject under consideration that I was not disconcerted.

"After these meetings were ended, Mr.

Moreland had an appointment to preach at a private house in another place. I went with him, and he insisted that I should preach, but I refused to do so. When the people had assembled he read, sung and led in prayer, and specially prayed for the young man who was about to address them. Thus I was compelled to preach, and I never afterward found so much diffidence in preaching as I had done. Mr. Moreland was one of the most devoted ministers that I ever knew, and was a striking monument of divine grace. He had been brought up as nearly in a state of heathenism as one could well be, in a civilized land, but God had mercy on him, and made him a chosen vessel to preach his gospel. Through the instrumentality of a lady, he was led to the house of God. He had a good memory, and he determined to let the lady see how much he could tell her about the sermon. He accordingly listened intently to the forenoon sermon, and was pursuing the same course in the afternoon, but before the preacher was through, he cried out aloud, with an awful sense of his sinfulness. His conversion was the result He afterward obtained an education and became an humble, laborious and successful minister of the gospel."

Mr. Rankin continued to labor in this field some four years, but toward its close the excitement on the slavery question became very warm in consequence of the admission of Missouri, into the Union, as a slave State. The feeling on this question, which was developed in Kentucky, convinced Mr. Rankin that he ought to carry out his first intention, and move to a free State. Nearly all the families in his congregation at Concord felt that the same course was their duty, and consequently they soon sold their farms, and moved to Indiana, where many of them with their descendants now reside. Mr. Rankin, however, carried out his first purpose of going to Ohio.

He arrived in Ripley in May, 1822, and became pastor of the church there, and of the congregation of Strait Creek, seven miles distant. He found this, at that period, a very hard field. Wickedness of ever kind abounded—frolicking, dancing, drinking and ball-playing were favorite pastimes.

Soon after his settlement some of the citizens began to complain of thefts being committed, and this led Mr. Rankin to attack drunkards and ball-players from the pulpit. He preached from the text: "Go to the ant, thou sluggard, and learn her ways, and be wise." He spoke of the sin and meanness of idleness and drinking, by which they were starving their families, and that some of them had even gone so far as to sell their wives, clothing for whisky. He affirmed that men who spend all their time drinking and playing ball must live off honest people, and that stealing had been done in the place was undeniable. This put an end to the ball-alley in Ripley.

At a communion season, soon after, he was so discouraged by the apparent coldness and deadness in his congregation that he determined to omit the usual appointment for preaching the following Monday. But on being told that the Rev. Mr. McCalla would be in town on Monday evening, he made an appointment for him, but he did not come. A considerable number of people gathered, and Mr. Rankin was constrained to preach, though he felt that he was very poorly prepared to do so. He selected for his text Rev. iii. 20 : "Behold, I stand at the door, and knock," etc. A large portion of the congregation was composed of the young and the careless of the community; and he pointed out to them the ways in which God had been knocking at the door of their hearts by his word, his ordinance, by his Spirit, and by his judgments, and referred to the fact that lately he had taken away by death several of their number—some of the wickedest men in the place. The appeal was blessed by the Spirit of God to the conviction of many of them of their sins, and in a few days they met in prayer-meeting to pray for one another, and the whole town seemed to be moved. Infidels came to church and seemed to hear with intense interest, and after few weeks he had a communion during which thirty were added to the church on profession of their faith. The work continued, and after some weeks, at a subsequent communion, twenty more were added. It was a conversion of sinners rather than a revival in the church. The work appeared, in a peculiar sense, the work of the Lord, and the result was very evident in the improved morality of the town.

A few of the fifty afterward went back, but only a few, the rest remained faithful, and many of them to this day are useful members of the Church, and good citizens in the State.

While thus encouraged to continue his labors in Ripley, and the way opened up for a long and useful pastorate, a new work was forced upon him—one for which we believe he had been specially prepared in the providence of God, viz : the discussion of the question of slavery, from a Bible standpoint. He says in a paper to the writer, "On the 2d of December, 1823, I received a letter from my brother Thomas, a merchant at Middlebrook, Va., informing me that he had purchased a slave. I immediately commenced a series of letters on the subject, and published them in the *Castigator*, then printed at Ripley, and sent him the paper. I afterward published them in book form. I had one thousand copies printed, but I was only able to bind a few of them at a time, so limited were my means. The printing cost me eighty dollars, which I paid by allowing the printer to occupy part of my house. In their preparation I was obliged to rely on the Bible for my arguments, as at that time anti-slavery works were few, and what there were was beyond my reach. The book when first published was well received, both in Kentucky and Ohio. Mr. Cox, bookseller at Maysville, Ky., several times supplied his store with it. Ohio was at that time an anti-slavery State, and there were many anti-slavery people in Kentucky, and in the other slave States. There were at that time abolition societies, both in the free and slave States. By these the sinfulness and consequent evils of slavery were discussed with a good deal of earnestness." Several causes seemed about this time to conspire to allay the agitation of the question of the sinfulness of slavery, and among them the occupation of the public mind with the question of colonization, so that abolition societies in the North became very few, and in the South ceased altogether. Mr. Rankin's book lay on the shelf for several years during this period; but a stray copy of it having fallen into the hands of William Loyd Garrison, was by him published in the *Liberator*. It was afterward made one of the standard books of the anti-slavery society and obtained a large circulation. Mr. Garrison acknowledged his indebtedness to Mr. Rankin for information contained in this volume, closing his letter thus: "With the profound and loving veneration of his anti-slavery disciple and humble co-worker in the cause of emancipation." In addition to this volume, Mr. Rankin published many tracts and articles in newspapers by which he hoped to enlighten the public mind and reach the conscience of the people in reference to the enormity of slavery, and among these, one urging the Government to set aside the public domain and use the proceeds of the sale of it for paying for the slaves. This plan was ridiculed by nearly every one. It was not believed that it was a possible thing to buy the slaves even if their masters had been willing to sell them. The possibility has however since then been demonstrated by our nation's expending a larger amount of money for the purpose of putting down the rebellion, than it would have cost to buy the slaves. It was well, however, that his plan was not adopted, for while it might have freed the slaves, it would not have secured them their rights as citizens, which they have now obtained. Nor would we have had the manifestation which we had, that God will punish national sin. During this period Mr. Rankin wrote other valuable books, and did much to promote the cause of temperance; but it does not fall within our plan to notice these volumes further than to say that his work entitled the "Covenant of Grace," has done much to promote right views on the important question of infant baptism.

He also devoted a portion of his time to the work of home missions, preaching in various places, in the log school-house, theaters and the sitting-rooms of farmers' houses—parlors had not then become fashionable. Through his instrumentality, six new churches were organized and eight houses of worship built, and nearly all the labor was done without compensation. He sought not earthly, but heavenly reward. It was seed time, and faithfully did he sow. He will doubtless come again with rejoicing, bringing his sheaves with him.

CHAPTER III.

THE BATTLE.

THE American Anti-slavery Society was organized in the city of New York, in 1833. Slavery was then beginning to become profitable in the South— the demand for cotton, and the improvements in the machinery used in getting it ready for the market, made it a profitable crop, and, as a matter of course, the desire of the slaveholder to retain and multiply the number of his slaves was increased. Many of them, however, had held their slaves hitherto with a troubled conscience, and they now began to hunt up arguments to silence their conscience, and justify their conduct to their fellow-men, and, strange to say, ministers of the gospel engaged in this nefarious project. The result was that both in the North and in the South the efforts of the anti-slavery men met with determined opposition, and just in proportion as their argument in defense of slavery was weak, did they show bitterness of spirit. In proportion as a man feels that the truth is on his side, is he forbearing to opposers. If he has confidence in his arguments he will not resort to hootings, hissings, and physical force, but the abettors of slavery had not very much confidence in their arguments, hence their resort to other means to sustain their cause. Mr. Rankin was employed by this society to lecture one year. He asked and obtained leave of his congregation to engage in this work, and commenced it by attending a meeting at Putnam, Ohio, called for the purpose of forming a State Anti-slavery Society. We will allow him to tell the story of his labors during the year in his own words. "At the meeting in Putnam a large mob was gathered together, and they threw stones at the building in which the convention held its meetings. The majority of the convention were peace men, and of course no resistance to the mob was made. There was an Englishman present, a preacher, of some order, against whom the mob vented their malice, because he was both an abolitionist and a foreigner. His name was Howels. He invited me to take tea with him. I locked arms with him, and we started for his house. The cry was raised, "Where is Howels? Where is Howels? And the mob surrounded us, as I suppose two hundred strong. A very large man came to Howe,s, gritting his teeth with rage and said to him, Do you want to see me? No, said Howels, I don't want to see you; I know nothing about you. Howels became afraid to go home lest the mob should tear down his house. We turned to go a different course. We had gone but a little distance when they hit Howels on the back with a rotten goose egg; but it fell on the ground before it broke, else it would have put us both in a bad condition. Another goose egg hit me on one shoulder; it also fell to the ground before it broke; it had a goslin in it about ready to come out. The mob then gathered the gravel that was in the street, and caused it to fall around us like hail. No harm was done. We passed into a house, and the mob had a fight among themselves. This was my first acquaintance with a mob. It is one of the worst forms in which human nature can appear. The aspect of a fierce mob is terrible.

"The convention was composed of all classes of Christian people. All demominational distinctions were lost, and the love and harmony that prevailed were such as I never witnessed before. The convention was large, and having transacted its business it adjourned. The mob did not venture to do more than throw stones at the house in which it held its sessions. A State Anti-slavery Society was formed. On my way home I staid over Sabbath at Chillicothe, and preached twice for the colored people. During the night service, a mob threw stones into the church, and hurt some persons. They designed to inflict violence on me, but a friend was with me who was a large and strong man, into contact with whom they did not like to come. These mobs were composed of an ignorant rabble who were made to believe that the design of the abolitionists was to get the poor white people and the negroes to marry together in order to make more servants. The belief of this infuriated them. This slander was put forth by Henry Clay, in the Senate of the United

States, in a speech, to which Thomas Morris made a noble reply. Clay designed by it to set the rabble of the nation on the abolitionists. He knew it was not true. Such consummate meanness ought to darken his reputation down to the end of time.

"When I commenced my course of lectures against slavery, the spirit of mobocracy was rife in almost every place. My first lecture was in a Methodist Church near Mowrystown, twenty-five miles from Ripley. The audience was not large, but was attentive; and I believe generally accorded with the sentiments of the lecture. There were some indications of mob spirit in the village, but there was no violence offered. The next place at which I lectured was Williamsburg. The Presbyterian minister at that place was a Mr. Gazley. He made strong opposition, and said publicly that my cause would bring on bloodshed and war upon the nation. I replied that his course was calculated to get up a mob. I lectured in the evening; the audience was attentive and manifested no disapprobation. As I was returning from the place in which I lectured, and was walking alone, without a light, a young man threw a stick with considerable force, and struck me on the neck. The night being very cold, I had put on three coats with heavy collars which shielded my neck from injury. The stick was round and about two feet long. Next morning one of the citizens persuaded the magistrate of the place to issue a warrant for him, but he ran off, and of course was not taken. The lecture was not in vain. Some of the citizens were ever after abolitionists, and some of them were zealous workers in the cause of liberty.

"From Williamsburg I went to Goshen. In that village the Presbyterian Church was opened for lectures, and the pastor was favorable. I lectured with success, and formed an anti-slavery society. Soon after the formation of this society, a fugitive slave came into the neighborhood, and hired himself to a man who, with his family, was prejudiced against colored people, but as work hands were not easily obtained he hired this black man. The fugitive behaved so well that the family became attached to him, and their prejudices passed away, and the fugitive was enabled to exercise confidence in them. He then told the gentleman who had employed him, that he was a fugitive slave, from the far South, and that he had been so long on the way that he had worn out his shoes, and clothes, and needed money to pay his expenses to Canada. The gentleman rode to Goshen, and told the abolitionists that there was a fugitive slave at his house, that he needed shoes, clothes, and money to pay his way through to Canada. The abolitionists furnished the shoes, clothes, and money needed. The gentleman took all these home and gave them to the fugitive, and the poor fellow was so overcome by the kindness shown him, in a strange land, that he wept like a child. He had no thought of there being any such white people in this hard-hearted world. It is better thus to aid the poor and helpless, than to have a kingdom in this world.

"I lectured with success at Batavia, the county-seat of Clermont County. At that place anti-slavery principles were propagated to considerable extent. Two miles from that place I had an appointment at night in a church. Whilst I was speaking, some fellows, of the baser sort, came to the door of the church, and threw eggs and stones at me; but without effect. The vile fellows hastily ran away, but the audience became alarmed and left. I urged them to stay, assuring them that I was the only one in danger ; but to no purpose. The people moved off, and left me to follow them. This was the only case in which I had my audience to leave without hearing me through. And this through sheer cowardice in the people; there was no danger of any of them being hurt.

"I lectured and preached, in a Baptist Church, five miles from New Richmond. In this neighborhood my letters on slavery had been read, and, consequently, there were abolitionists there. The Baptist brethern received me kindly. I was with them on the Sabbath day. I preached for them, and they heard me gladly. In this neighborhood abolitionism was triumphant.

"A few miles distant there was a Presbyterian Church at which I lectured and preached with success. Anti-slavery sentiments prevailed in all the congregation. At this time my brother, Alexander T. Rankin, was pastor of the Presbyterian Church at Felicity. My brother invited me to come and lecture in his church. I made an appointment to lecture on a certain evening, during a meeting of the Cincinnati Presbytery, at that place. The elders of the church of Felicity refused to let me have the use of the house, and the Methodists let me have the use of their house. The fact that I was refused the use of the house—that I had been the instrumental cause of its being built, stirred up the people, and the Methodist Church was filled with hearers, and the members of the Cincinnati Presbytery attended. After the lecture sixty names were given in for the formation of an anti-slavery society. The elders who refused to let me have the use of the church were not pro-slavery men, but thought it was inexpedient to have a lecture of that kind in the church. They did not in this case represent the sentiments of the church. The church no doubt would have voted me the use of the house, if they had been called upon to decide in the case.

I lectured at West Union, in the Presbyterian Church, and formed a large anti-slavery society; but the pastor gave it no encouragement, and of course it ceased to exist, and West Union became so pro-slavery, that several of the ministers of Ripley Presbytery, because they were abolitionists, had their horses shaved, during a meeting of Presbytery at that place. This was done by the baser sort of men; but had it not been a pro-slavery place, that class of fellows would not have committed such an outrage upon respectable clergymen. I told the pastor of the Presbyterian Church, that he was responsible for that shameful conduct; that if he had done his duty no such thing would have happened. Some of the citizens felt very sensibly that the village was disgraced. My horse escaped, by being locked in a stable.

A large anti-slavery meeting was held at Winchester, in a grove. A considerable mob was collected, and, at times, beat drums so that nothing could be heard. A rowdy old fellow forced himself upon the stand, and delivered a ludicrous speech. While I was speaking, a man by the name of Stivers, about drunk enough to do mischief, came in front with a large club, drawn with both hands, to strike me. A gentleman arose up between us, and let him know that he would have to strike more than one if he persisted in his design. He desisted from offering violence. When our meeting closed some of the mob were so drunk that they could not get off the ground, and were left lying in the grove. As I was riding out of the village, and passing a tavern, a young fellow pitched at me a large batch of eggs, designing to cover me with the contents; but he was not philosopher enough to calculate for the motion of the horse. The eggs passed behind me and over the horse without touching, and fell harmlessly in the street. I said to him, 'That was a mistake,' and passed on.

"Next day after the meeting at Winchester, one was held at Decatur, and a mob appeared there in force ; but some men came to the meeting armed, and were determined to use their arms in case the mob should attempt any violence, and by that means peace was secured. The best class of the citizens of that village were, at that time, anti-slavery. Decatur has since become one of the most anti-slavery and moral villages in the State.

A friend of mine made an appointment for me to lecture at Withamsville, on the road from Georgetown to Cincinnati. My friend went with me. We lodged with an acquaintance of his, and who was a mobacrat. The lecture was in the evening, at a school-house. A wild looking set of young men were the audience. I waited some time, hoping that some old men would come in, but none came. In the meantime a stone was thrown upon the roof of the school-house. At length some one said that it was time to commence the lecture. I replied that I would be happy to address them, if they were disposed to hear, and if they were not disposed to hear, it would be no use for me to attempt to address them. I inquired who threw that stone upon the house. The reply was that no one knew. I began my lecture, and fixed my eyes upon the worst looking fellows, and kept them still, so long as I could look them in the eye; but they turned their backs to me, and were disposed to misbehave. I talked to them, and kept them in order as well as I could, until I got through.

THE BATTLE. 49

Then they began to blackguard and use the most obscene language. They gathered up the burning fire-brands and followed us on the way to our lodging, and threw them at us. The man with whom we lodged was struck first, and then I was struck next on the shoulder with a burning fire-brand, but the force of it was expended before it struck me, so that it did no injury. They swore most profanely, and threatened vengeance in case I should go into their township to lecture. After all the arguments I could use to show that all men ought to be free, it did seem, as if there were some men who were not fit for freedom. Such a demonstration was the strongest argument that could be formed against the freedom of all men. Creatures so vile and so wicked as those young men at Withamsville were, did not seem fit to be free. I discovered by actual experiment that more could be accomplished by preaching than by lecturing. A solemn discourse foundde on the Scriptures had an authority, and a divine sanction, that a mere lecture could not have, and there was less danger of disturbance by mobs. I adopted the plan of preaching and mingling the subject of slavery with other gospel subjects. In this way I could bring my hearers to view faith in the light of eternity. The pastor of the Presbyterian Church at Springdale, Ohio, Rev. A. Aten, had himself right views on slavery, and desired to have the people of his own charge enlightened on that subject. Several lectures had been delivered there by able men with little effect. I proposed to him to appoint a communion which he agreed to do. I attended on the occasion. I preached on Friday and Saturday, in as solemn and earnest a manner as I could do, and said nothing about slavery. On Sabbath morning, before the communion, I preached on a text enforcing humility and benevolence. I presented Christ as the great example. I exhibited his condescension and benevolence in the most earnest manner of which I was capable. All the benevolent principles of anti-slavery were presented in a strong light; but slavery was not mentioned. At the close of the communion I gave notice that in the evening I would give them the Bible views of slavery; that I would not say anything inconsistent with the Sabbath, but would just carry out the benevolent principles of the forenoon discourse. The evening audience was large. I vindicated the Scriptures from the foul charge of giving sanction to slavery, and showed that the Bible condemned all oppression of which slavery is the worst form. On Monday I preached again, and said nothing about slavery. In the evening I addressed them again on slavery, and formed an anti-slavery society of sixty members. No opposition was made. And there was a deep interest manifested as if there were a revival of religion. I visited other Presbyterian Churches, and preached in the same way with equal success.

"I served the American Anti-slavery Society six months, during which time I visited many places and propagated anti-slavery principles extensively. I believe that I never, but in one case, addressed an audience without producing the conviction that what I said was true; but it was more difficult to produce the belief that I taught abolitionism. After the discourse was closed it was sometimes said, 'Why, is that abolitionism? Why, if that is abolitionism, I am an abolitionist; that is all right; but surely that can't be it; Birney teaches a different doctrine from that.' Sometimes at public meetings I made appointments, and invited all to come and hear, assuring them that they would agree with me in sentiment

At such appointments I commenced by stating what I believed.

"1. I believe that 'all men are created equal, and endowed with certain unalienable rights, among which are life, liberty, and the pursuit of happiness.' They surely believed this, for it was in the Declaration of Independence.

"2. I believed that God 'made of one blood all nations of men.' They surely believed this, for it is in the Bible.

"3. I believe that every man ought either to do his own work or pay the man for it who does it. As honest men they surely believed this. The Savior said, 'The laborer is worthy of his reward.' These are the doctrines maintained by abolitionists. They contend that such are rights of all men regardless of color. It was the application of these doctrines to a great system of painful oppression that excited so violent opposition to abolitionists, and not any error in their doctrines which were just those held by our revolutionary fathers, and clearly expressed in the Declaration of Independence. Hence I never failed, when fairly heard, to produce the conviction that what I said was true.

"By labor and exposure I was reduced so that I was obliged to quit the service of the society. I took cold, which brought on a severe cough, under which I suffered during some months. I did not expect to recover; but by the good providence of God I regained my health. Since that time more than thirty years have passed away, and still I live and have health. Thanks be to the Giver of all good.

"Some years since, at the request of friends, I spent one month in the State of Indiana, speaking against slavery. My efforts there were in general well received.

"Mr. John Rankin, of Chester County, Pennsylvania, wrote me a letter inviting me to come and labor in his section of country on the subject of slavery, and promised to pay my traveling expenses. I accepted his invitation, and at the end of a long and pleasant journey I arrived at his house and found a very kind and pleasant family. I began my labors in the midst of opposition. Several Presbyterian ministers, even, set themselves against me with a zeal that in a good cause would have brought them great honor. They exerted their influence to exclude me from houses in which to hold meetings. There was one exception. I did preach once in the church of which Mr. Rankin was a member, and this had a tendency to give me hearers at other places. There were many Hicksite Quakers in that region, and they had put up a hall for the purpose of having anti-slavery lectures. In that hall I held meetings. The Quakers heard me gladly, although I delivered truths that contravened their belief. A young Quaker, after hearing me, fell sick and soon died.

I visited him on his dying bed. He was a man of talents and influence. I conversed with him as a sick man; he was pleased with my conversation, and said 'he would hear me on anything.' At various places Quakers and Infidels came to hear me preach, and I delivered them the truths adapted to their condition. I presented to them in strong terms the fundamental truths of the gospel, and the evidences of the inspiration of the Scriptures, and yet I was heard with interest. A Quaker said to an Old School minister, 'If thee did preach as John Rankin does I would not go past thy church to my own. I would hear thee.' I appointed to hold a meeting on Sabbath at Oxford in a grove. It rained so that we could not occupy the grove. Near to the grove was a large new barn, owned by a colored man. It was without a floor, and the lower story was used for a stable. The people assembled in this stable, and I preached to them on the subject of slavery. I had a considerable audience. I remarked that we were not so comfortably situated as might be desired; but it should be remembered that the Savior was born in a stable. I gave the Bible view of slavery, and vindicated the Scriptures from the foul charge of giving sanction to slavery. An Infidel who heard me said " he did not before believe that the Bible could be so vindicated.' By hearing pro-slavery ministers preach he had been made believe that the Bible did justify holding slaves. For Monday evening we had the promise of a schoolhouse in the village of Oxford, and an appointment was made; the people assembled at the hour, and found it locked against them, and it was dark, and no entrance could be obtained. I said to the people, if you can stand to hear I can preach to you by starlight. They consented, and I preached with no other light than what emanated from the stars. I labored one month in Chester and Lancaster Counties, and delivered nearly forty discourses. On one occasion eggs were thrown at me, and an old lady was hit on the breast with one, and was hurt by it; but I was not hit. The result of my labors was the formation of a Free Presbyterian Church which still exists. My friend John Rankin has since gone to rest.

"I will now give one of my most effective anti-slavery sermons. Phil. ii. 5:

"'If there be, therefore, any consolation in Christ, if any comfort of love, if any fellowship of the Spirit, if any vowels and mercies, fulfill ye my joy, that ye be like-minded, having the same love, being of one accord, of one mind. Let nothing be done through strife or vainglory; but in lowliness of mind let each esteem others better than themselves. Look not every man on his own things, but every man also on the things of others. Let this mind be in you, which was also in Christ Jesus.'

"This is one of the most pathetic appeals ever made. It was addressed to a people that had been brought up in a state of heathenism, the tendency of which is to abolish all the finer feelings of our nature. 'Hence the dark places of the earth are full of the habitations of cruelty.' It is truly affirmed that the heathen are 'destitute of natural affection.' Infidels tell us that Christians ought to go to China to learn morals, and yet in one city of that empire not less than ten thousand infants were annually thrown into the streets to perish! In the most enlightened periods of heathen Rome there were laws prescribing the manner in which weakly and diseased infants should be put to death. We who live in this Christian country, where the term mother is significant of tenderness and love, can not fully feel the force of this appeal.

"In all ages of the world there has been in our fallen nature a tendency to division. This tendency was felt in the apostolic churches. The design of the apostle in this appeal was that of urging the church of Philippi to Christian unity. If they had experienced any consolation in union with Christ, that ought to induce them to exercise love to their Christian brethren. And what in this sorrowful world is so consoling as a consciousness of union with Christ so as to be justified by his righteousness, and sanctified by the spirit he has procured by his merits? He who is in Christ has that hope 'which is both sure and steadfast, and which entereth into that which is within the vail.' He is an heir of God, and a joint-heir with Christ. He has strong consolation having fled for refuge to the court of the Savior's righteousness, under which no one ever perished.

"If they had felt any comfort of love, that ought to be a strong motive to Christian unity. And what is there this side of heaven that gives so much comfort as love? Supreme love to God and appropriate love to our fellow-beings can make us truly happy. If love were banished from this world there could be no rational enjoyment; miserable would be the condition of all rational beings. It is love that constitutes the happiness of heaven. Without love there could be no heaven. Angels bereft of love would be devils.

"If they enjoyed the fellowship of the Spirit, that ought to prompt them to live in holy union. All true Christians are born of the Spirit, and have a common interest in the Holy Ghost. He dwells in all who have union with the Savior, and therefore they ought to be united in love.

"If any bowels and mercies had resulted from union with Christ, that ought to excite them to exercise that holy love of the brethren which secures the unity that ought to exist among the followers of the Savior. The tendency of the religion of Christ is to implant benevolence in the human heart, and purify and soften our nature. 'The wisdom that is from above is first pure, then peaceable, gentle, easy to be entreated, full of mercy and good fruits, without partiality, and without hypocrisy.' James iii. 17. 'Pure religion and undefiled before God and the Father is this: to visit the fatherless and widows in their affliction, and to keep himself unspotted from the world.' James i. 27. These passages describe Christianity as a system of true benevolence and moral purity. The man who has no compassion for his fellow-men has no just claim to being united to the benevolent Son of God.

"The church of Philippi was gathered by Paul out of heathenism, and was transformed into Christian life by divine influences. This glorious change filled the apostle with joyful anticipations. Hence he entreated them to fulfill his joy, being 'like-minded, having the same love, being of one accord, of one mind.' This unity was essential both to their happiness and prosperity. In order to secure this unity there must be—

"1. The exercise of humility. 'Let nothing be done through strife or vainglory; but in lowliness of mind let each esteem others better than themselves.' 'Of pride only cometh contention.' All pride is sinful and never tends to good. Some parents teach their children that they ought to have so much pride as to keep them out of bad company and from low and mean conduct; pride has no such tendency; it is itself one of the meanest things in the universe. The proudest men on earth are the men we may expect to do the meanest things. The Devil is the proudest being in the universe, and yet he does the meanest things. It was pride that prompted his revolt in heaven. If pride could now enter heaven, it would produce turmoil and ruin there as it does on earth; all the lower orders would envy the higher, and there would be war in heaven. While we should not abandon a good cause because men will make strife if we adhere to it, yet we ought not to carry a good cause for the purpose of making strife, nor should we do anything for self aggrandizement. And if we will notice carefully the evil thoughts and propensities of our own hearts we may readily esteem others better than ourselves.

"2. In order to secure unity there must be the exercise of benevolence. 'Look not every man on his own things, but every man also on the things of others.' We must not so look upon our own interests as to neglect the interests of others. We must aim to promote the welfare of all our fellow-beings so far as opportunity offers. This is in accordance with the moral law, 'Thou shalt love thy neighbor as thyself.' This does not mean that we must feel toward our neighbor that warmth of passion which we feel toward our wives and children, relatives and intimate friends. We feel no such passion toward ourselves. We feel a constant desire for our own welfare and happiness, and to fulfill the law of love we must feel the same constant desire for the welfare and happiness of our neighbor. And what is due to our neighbor, in this respect, is due to all others. 'All things whatsoever ye would that men should do to you, do ye even so to them; for this is the law and the prophets.' No man can love his neighbor as himself, and speak those things with respect to his neighbor that he would not have spoken with respect to himself. The exercise of this love would prevent all slander, and thus abolish a prominent source of human misery. No man can love his neighbor as himself, and designedly overreach him in a bargain. The exercise of this love would banish all dishonest dealing from the world, and save millions from poverty and want. This would not injure the commerce of the world. It would not prevent the dealer from a reasonable percentage on his goods. No man can love his neighbor as himself and hold him in a position in which he would not be held himself. The exercise of this love would banish all slavery and oppression from the world. Enslaving men and holding them as property is wholly inconsistent with the laws of love. No man is willing to be a slave, and therefore no man can rightfully hold another man as a slave. What he would not have done to himself, he can not rightfully do to another. The law of love written upon every heart so that it would be obeyed, would banish from the world slavery and oppression, murder and theft, bloodshed and war, and every other species of crime. Under the universal influence of this love the whole world would become as the paradise of God, and sorrow and sighing would for ever pass away.

"3. Christ is presented as the great example of humility and benevolence. 'Let this mind be in you which was also in Christ Jesus.' To understand what the mind of Christ is, we must view him in his wonderful condescension. He was exalted above the heavens, and he 'being in the form of God, thought it not robbery to be equal with God; but made himself of no reputation, and took upon him the form of a servant, and was made in the likeness of man; and being formed in fashion as a man, he humbled himself, and became obedient unto death, even the death of the cross.' To be in the form of God is to be in his nature. If he had not been in the nature of God, he would have been a servant, and therefore could not have taken upon him the nature of a servant. He is the express image of the Father's person. An express image is an exact likeness. To be the exact likeness of the Father's person he must possess all divine perfections as fully as they are possessed by the Father's person. The Father is eternal, and if the Son were not eternal he would be infinitely unlike the Father. He is the Father's equal, and in him dwells 'the fullness of the Godhead bodily.' He is 'The mighty God, the everlasting Father.' Let us in imagination rise to the world of light and glory, and there behold the Son of God lighting up heaven in all its magnificence and grandeur. The highest intelligences around the throne of God vail their faces in his presence, and ascribe unto him glory, honor, power and dominion for ever and ever. Let us go back to the morning of creation and behold him throwing from his hand all the massy worlds that revolve on high, and by his word lighting up the vast universe; and now let us go to Bethlehem and see him a helpless babe in a stable, lying in a manger, out of which beasts had been fed. All heaven is filled with wonders. What infinite condescension! He who was infinitely higher than the heavens, took our nature into connection with his divine nature, so as to unite the two natures in one person forever. Here is the grandest truth in the universe. Angels never saw so much of God before. Never did they before strike so high a note of praise. 'Glory to God in the highest, on earth peace, good will to men,' was their song when the Savior was born. He who created and owned the whole universe, became poorer than foxes of the mountains, and the birds of the air. 'The foxes have holes, and the birds of the air have nests, but the Son of man hath not where to lay his head." The stable was his birthplace, and the manger was his cradle! His companions were poor fishermen, and to the poor he preached the gospel. He girded himself with a towel and washed his disciples' feet. Come, ye who despise your fellow-men, because they were born in a foreign country, or because they are poor or uneducated, or have a colored skin, and view the condescension of the Son of God. He condescended to take the nature you despise in your fellow-men, and to wear it for ever. He never despised a human being. He will permit the lowest and darkest of our race, redeemed by his blood, to sit with him in his own throne. Hear his declaration. 'To him that overcometh will I grant to sit with me in my throne, even as I also overcame, and am set down with my Father in his throne.' Rev. iii. 21. You will not permit the colored man to sit with you at your table, or in the house of God; but he, who is Lord of lords and King of kings, will permit him to sit with himself on his own throne! 'Now if any man have not the spirit of Christ, he is none of his.' You can not get to heaven with a proud heart that leads you to despise your fellow-men. There is no such pride in heaven. The holy angels, of higher nature than we are, condescend to attend to the lowest of our race. The beggar Lazarus was as loathsome as a human being could be. He was full of sores, and had nothing to cover them. He lay neglected and starving at the rich man's gate. The holy angels came from heaven, and took care of this poor beggar; and when he died they carried his spirit on wings of love to Abraham's bosom. Oh, how lovely is such benevolence! Such you must have, or you can not inherit the kingdom of God. It was benevolence that caused the Son of God to assume our nature, and endure the shameful death of the cross, and all the sufferings necessary to meet the demands of justice. He is our great example of humility and benevolence. Let us follow him in doing good to our fellow-men. Let us be willing to go down and do the lowest service in Christ's kingdom, and labor to elevate the lowest of our race, that they may become the sons and daughters of the Almighty."

This sermon was preached frequently by Mr. Rankin, both in the East and in the West. As it was not written but preached extempore, it was somewhat varied in different places, and it was generally well received. The impression produced was that the abolitionists were not so reckless and unreasonable as they had been represented. The battle was fairly begun on the one side by argument and appeals to the plain teaching of the Scriptures, and on the other by misrepresentation, vituperation and persecution. Mr. Rankin's decided stand made him specially obnoxious to the defenders of the peculiar institution. Many false and slanderous reports were circulated concerning him, and large rewards were offered for him in Kentucky. After the great mob in Cincinnati against the negroes, a number of men came to Mr. Rankin's house one night, at Ripley, with the purpose of taking his life, but his sons had taken the precaution to prepare themselves for such visits, and though a good deal of shooting was done, no serious consequences resulted. The Keeper of Israel preserved him for further work in his vineyard. This question of slavery now became the great question, not only in the State but also in the Church, nor could it be excluded from the large benevolent societies in the land. The slavery propagandists obtained complete control in national affairs, and used their power to crush out, as far as possible, every aspiration of our citizens after the equal rights of men. Abolitionists were branded as infidels, and charged with trampling under their feet the plainest teachings of Scripture. The Fugitive Slave bill was enacted into a law, and the entire North thereby made slave hunting ground, and our citizens liable at any moment to be made slave catchers under the severest penalties. Finally, the Missouri Compromise was repealed with the avowed purpose of extending the accursed system into our heretofore free Territory. No man who dared oppose the behests of the slave power at this period could hope for advancement either in Church or State, and the charitable associations that dared to speak against it, must, as far as their fiat was concerned, be allowed to starve. And such was the influence of this determined spirit that nearly all bowed before the power and allowed the seal of silence to be placed on their lips. It was then that Mr. Rankin made an effort to organize the American Reform, now the Western Tract and Book Society. After corresponding with several anti-slavery friends in reference to the matter, he issued a call for a meeting that they might organize a Tract Society that would not be afraid to publish against that "dominating system of oppression" so powerful in the land. The meeting was held in Vine Street Congregational Church, December 16, 1851. A Tract Society was resolved upon and Mr. Rankin was chosen President, and Dr. Boynton, Corresponding Secretary. It was soon found that the mere organization of a Society would accomplish nothing unless funds were obtained to enable it to carry its purpose, and this was the great desideratum in this case, for few churches would open their doors to allow an appeal to be made in its behalf, and, as the result, it could not obtain such agents as it desired to labor in its behalf. Mr. Rankin was obliged to undertake the work himself, and was, in view of all the circumstances, very successful—to him more than any other one man, this Society owes its existence and present prosperity. Ever since its formation he has had the honor of being annually elected its President, and every year has he shown his interest in its work by devoting part of his time to presenting its claims among the churches. Small and despised once, it has nevertheless held on its way until it is now recognized as an institution not only of Cincinnati, but of the West. Its record is a proud one. Nearly the entire nation now acknowledges that its course was the true one, and it is not too much to say that it has done more than any other institution in the land to enlighten our citizens respecting the enormity of the crime of slavery, and thus to prepare them during our late terrible contest to break the chains of the oppressed. If this had been the entire work of Mr. Rankin's life, we believe that he would have accomplished far more than most men are privileged to do; but this is only part of his labor. It is, however, a part that will doubtless long continue after he has gone to his rest, and concerning it he may be able to say with joyful tongue: "They rest from their labors, and *their works do follow them.*" Mr. Rankin furnished to the Society several of its best tracts on slavery and kindred subjects. We subjoin one still of immense importance to us as a nation.

DUTY OF VOTING FOR RIGHTEOUS MEN FOR OFFICE.

Christ is the Supreme Ruler and Lawgiver;

Civil government is his ordinance;

Its officers are his ministers, and therefore they should be just men;

Voters are his appointing agents, and are held responsible to him for the votes they give.

I. Christ is the Supreme Ruler and Lawgiver. To him is "given dominion and glory, and a kingdom, that all people, nations and languages should serve him. His dominion is an everlasting dominion, which shall not pass away; and his kingdom that which shall not be destroyed." Dan. vii. 14. This shows clearly that his authority over all nations is supreme. He is the "stone cut out of the mountain without hands," that shall break in pieces and consume all kingdoms that oppose his reign. Dan. ii. 34, 35, 44. "The kings of the earth set themselves, and the rulers take counsel together against the Lord, and against his anointed, saying, Let us break their bands asunder, and cast away their cords from us." Ps. ii. 2, 3. Here the kings and rulers are represented as conspiring against his authority; but, in despite of them, the Father determined to place his Son upon the throne, and to give the nations into his hand. "Yet have I set my king upon my holy hill of Zion. Ask me, and I shall give thee the heathen for thine inheritance, and the uttermost parts of the earth for thy possession. Thou shalt break them with a rod of iron; thou shalt dash them in pieces, like a potter's vessel. Be wise now, therefore, O ye kings; be instructed, ye judges of the earth; serve the Lord with fear, and rejoice with trembling. Kiss the Son, lest he be angry, and ye perish from the way, when his wrath is kindled but a little." Ps. ii. 6, 8, 12. Such are the ancient predictions respecting the dominion of Christ over all nations. The nations are rightfully his, both by creation and redemption. Hence, " the government shall be upon his shoulders." Isa. ix. 6. " To him is given all power in heaven and in earth." Matt. xxviii. 18. He is the " only Potentate, the King of kings, and Lord of lords." 1 Tim. vi. 15. " At the name of Jesus every knee should bow, of things in heaven, and things in earth, and things under the earth." Phil. ii. 10. " For he is Lord of lords, and King of kings." Rev. xvii. 14. These sacred passages most clearly prove that Christ is the Supreme Ruler and Lawgiver, and that all nations and their rulers are placed under his authority. And consequently, he should be acknowledged, in every civil constitution, as the rightful ruler of all nations.

II. Civil government is Christ's ordinance. "The powers that be are ordained of God; whosoever, therefore, resisteth the power, resisteth the ordinance of God." Rom. xiii. 1, 2. God gave to men all the rights necessary to the enjoyment of happiness in the present life, and he ordained civil government to secure to them the free exercise of those rights. All the principles of right by which men are to be governed, are clearly revealed in the sacred oracles. Love is to be the governing principle in all legislation. "Thou shalt love thy neighbor as thyself." "Love worketh no ill to his neighbor." "All things whatsoever ye would that men should do to you, do ye even so to them; for this is the law and the prophets." These short sentences contain all the rules necessary to a just legislation. The legislator should be guided by the law of love in all his legislation. This will secure the infliction of due punishment for the crimes that injure society, and promote misery among men. Love to the whole requires the just punishment of criminals. Civil government is of vast importance, and greatly promotes the welfare of all classes of human beings, when rightfully exercised. Hence, its authority should be duly regarded ; and it should be esteemed as one of Heaven's best gifts to men.

III. Civil officers are Christ's ministers, and therefore they should be just men. Paul says of the civil magistrate, that "he is the minister of God to thee for good." And that "he is the minister of God, a revenger to execute wrath upon him that doeth evil." Rom. xiii. 4. And he urges the duty of paying tribute, on the ground that magistrates " are God's ministers." Rom. xiii. 6. In view of these inspired declarations, it is presumed that none will deny that civil officers are Christ's ministers ; and it follows that they ought to be just men, who will render to God and man what is due. This conclusion is fully sustained by the voice of inspiration : " Thou shalt provide out of all the people able men, such as fear God, men of truth, hating covetousness ; and place such over them, to be rulers. And Moses chose able men out of all Israel, and made them heads over the people." Exod. xviii. 21, 25. " The God of Israel said, the Rock of Israel spake to me, He that ruleth over men must be just, ruling in the fear of God ; and he shall be as the light of the morning when the sun riseth, even a morning, without clouds." 2 Sam. xxiii. 3, 4. " Rulers are not a terror to good works, but to the evil. The ruler is a minister of God for good ; a revenger to execute wrath upon him that doeth evil." Rom. xiii. 3, 4. Thus the sacred oracles fully sustain the conclusion that civil officers should be just men, spotless in character, as the morning without clouds.

IV. Voters are Christ's appointing agents, and are held responsible to him for the votes they give. In the United States, the officers are elected by the people; consequently, the voters are Christ's appointing agents, to appoint the civil rulers who are to be his ministers for good. Now, if it be Christ's will, that just men fearing God, and men of truth, should be appointed, is it not the duty of the voters, who, by his providence, are made his agents, to appoint such? Can any one possibly doubt that it is Christ's will, that righteous men should be appointed to legislate, and administer justice? And if there can be no doubt respecting his will, there can be none in respect to the duty of voting for such as he wills to be in office. The obligation to vote for just men to be rulers, may be enforced by a variety of considerations.

1. It is clearly the will of Christ that men should thus vote, whether they be professors of religion or not. All are bound to regard his will. He has a rightful claim to the services of all, as the creatures of his power. He commands "all men, everywhere, to repent." The obligation to obey Christ lies upon all men; none can escape from his power and authority. Hence, all shall answer to him, at the judgment-seat, for every vote given.

2. To vote for wicked men to fill civil offices is to corrupt the ordinance of God. And will Christ hold the man guiltless, that corrupts an important ordinance of God, and one designed to secure the welfare and happiness of millions of rational beings? Just in proportion to the vast importance of civil government is the magnitude of the sin of voting for wicked men.

3. Voting for wicked men makes them

Christ's ministers and thus profanes the offices he has ordained for the protection of the innocent, and the punishment of the vicious. Is not such voting highly criminal, and most offensive to God ? Is it not one of the works that God will bring into judgment ?

4. Voting for wicked men justifies them in their wickedness ; and " He that justifieth the wicked—is an abomination to the Lord." Prov. xvii. 15. Is it a light matter for a man so to cast his vote, as to make himself an abomination to the Lord ?

5. Voting for wicked men causes the people to mourn : " When the righteous are in authority, the people rejoice ; but when the wicked beareth rule, the people mourn." Prov. xxix. 2. " As a roaring lion, and a ranging bear, so is a wicked ruler over the poor people." Prov. xxviii. 15. Wicked rulers pervert justice, and bring calamity upon the people. Of this

we have a shocking specimen in the fugitive slave enactment by Congress; by which thousands of innocent people were driven from their houses and homes into a foreign land, there to endure starvation and want; and by which, innocent and helpless men are, in the heart of this professedly Christian country, torn from their wives and children, and driven into perpetual slavery. Under this barbarous enactment, the whole land mourns, so far as humane feeling extends. Under it every compassionate heart bleeds, and every benevolent bosom throbs with anguish. And yet how many professors of religion voted for the wicked men who formed this cruel enactment. And how much greater number of such voted for men to fill the office of the presidency, who had pledged themselves to sustain this wicked and grievous enactment! Surely such voters must meet, at the judgment-seat of Christ, all the oppressions resulting from their votes. All the wicked and cruel enactments of the States and general government are the results of voting for wicked men; and consequently the voters are responsible for all the governmental oppressions of the United States. What a long and dreadful account must be given at the judgment-seat of Christ, respecting the millions that have perished and are now perishing, by the oppressions of this nation! What an astounding fact it is, that there are in this Christian nation more than three millions of people with respect to whom there is not one sentence of law to protect the marriage rite, nor the family relations; and who are prohibited, by severe penalties, from learning to read the word of life. They are bought and sold, as if they were beasts of the field! What floods of tears daily water the face of the ground! What agonizing groans hourly ascend to heaven! And what streams of blood flow from the scourged and tortured bodies! All these tears, groans and streams of blood must be met in the day of judgment, by all the voters who have sustained, and those who do now sustain this horrible system of oppression. Every one of them "shall give an account of himself to God." Rom. xiv. 12.

6. Voting for wicked men tends to increase wickedness. The wicked example of rulers has great influence on the masses of the people, and is calculated to encourage them to engage in vicious practices. "The wicked walk on every side, when the vilest men are exalted." Ps. xii. 8. Therefore, he that votes for wicked men, is a promoter of wickedness, and must answer for it when he comes to judgment.

7. Voting for wicked men endangers our republican institutions. Men who do not fear God are ever liable, when in power, to oppress the people, and to turn

a republic into a military despotism. The late President ordered out the military to enforce, against the consciences and humanity of the people of Boston, the fugitive slave enactment; and thus far made the government a military despotism, and that of the worst form. Who does not know, that a few hundred thousand slaveholders control the general government, and that they have made us a nation of slave-catchers? Under their denomination, the government has commanded us to do the most cruel and degrading service under heaven. What can be more cruel than to catch the panting fugitive, and deliver him over to torments lifelong? And what can be more degrading than to take rank with bloodhounds? Can a republic, that thus degrades its citizens, be long sustained? All this tyranny and degradation are the results of voting for wicked men, who have no fear of God before their eyes.

8. It must be admitted that it is the duty of all to pray that God may give the nation good rulers; but to pray thus, and then vote for adulterers and fornicators, for duelists and slaveholders, as many professors of religion have done, is a heaven-daring sin. We should not thus provoke God to anger. If it be our duty to pray that God may give us good rulers it is our duty to vote for righteous men who fear God and hate covetousness.

9. Voting for wicked men will, if continued, ultimately so corrupt the nation, and involve it in crime, as to cause God either to abandon it to self-destruction, or to inflict upon it the most dreadful and destructive judgments, as he did upon Israel of old. Our national sins far transcend theirs in number and magnitude. It may be said, in respect to us, as it was in respect to them, " Shall I not visit for these things, saith the Lord; shall not

my soul be avenged on such a nation as this ? Jer. v. 9.

10. By voting just men into office, the nation may be reformed, and all unjust and sinful enactments may be abolished, and the best interests of all classes of people may be secured. Let just men be put in office, and the government will soon be relieved from the evils that now threaten its destruction, and disturb the peace of the nation. There is no one point in which the Church and nation more certainly need reform than in that of voting. This important privilege has been greatly abused by professors of religion, as well as by others. This is the prominent source of the deplorable oppressions and evils that now exist in our country; and nothing but reformation can save this mighty nation from the most terrible ruin. Will not all denominations of Christians unite their efforts and their influence to secure the election of

just men to office? We should not be deterred by the cry of uniting Church and State. Where so many denominations exist, there can be no danger of any such union ever taking place. There is vastly more danger of uniting Infidelity and the State. Let wicked and designing men raise that cry, if they choose, in order to secure to themselves the offices of the government, and carry on their oppressions, as they have done in times past; but let Christians be faithful to Him who will rule all rebellious nations with a rod of iron, and will dash in pieces all tyrannical kingdoms. We should not vote for wicked men, to sustain the better party.

We must not do evil, that good may come; nor choose to commit the least of two sins, by voting for one wicked man, in preference to another that is worse. If it be a sin to vote for a wicked man, we must not commit that sin to secure any good that may result. We should give our votes as religiously as we pray. We should have no politics but such as come from God; and all we do should be done to his glory.

If all the Christian denominations will but unite in voting for good men, *slavery can be abolished, and the sighing millions now in bondage can be set free; intemperance and Sabbath-breaking can, to a great extent, be banished from the land, and thousands now sitting in sadness, degradation, and want, can be elevated and made happy. Were this nation redeemed from the sin and disgrace of slavery, a sighing world would rejoice, and angels might sing anew, " Glory to God in the highest, and on earth peace, good-will toward men."

---
*Slavery is abolished, but the argument is good against other national sin, such as intemperance and Sabbath-breaking

CHAPTER IV.

INCIDENTS ON THE BATTLE-FIELD.

THE love of liberty seems to be implanted in the nature of men. " Give me liberty or give me death" is an expression which touches a chord in every human heart. The comforts of life can not be enjoyed unless sweetened by liberty. Hence the great sacrifices that men in every age have made to obtain liberty for themselves and to transmit it to their posterity; and we might also add the pleasure that good men, who enjoy liberty themselves, find in helping their less favored fellow-men to obtain it. We have an illustration and also proof of these truths in the fact that so many colored men at great risk of suffering, and even death, escaped from their bondage, and were helped by abolitionists, also at great risk, on their way to Canada by what was familiarly termed the underground railway—called such because the work was done at night secretly, one neighbor taking a fugitive to another neighbor where he lay hid all next day, and then the following night pursued his journey again until he found a safe resting-place. There was no organization to secure this result; men acted spontaneously as the cases arose. Mr. Rankin, as was well known at the time, was largely engaged in this work. We give a few of the incidents as noted down by his own pen, and we doubt not some of our readers will say of them, "Truth is stranger than fiction:"

"I kept a depot on what was called the underground railway. It was so called because they who took passage on it disappeared from public view as really as if they had gone into the ground. After

THE BATTLE. 97

the fugitive slaves entered a depot on that road, no trace of them could be found. They were secretly passed from one depot to another until they arrived in Canada. This road extended its branches through all the free States. These were formed without any general concert. There was no secret society organized. There were no secret oaths taken, nor promises of secrecy extorted. And yet there were no betrayals. Anti-slavery persons were actuated by sense of humanity and right, and, of course, were true to one another. It may seem incredible that lines over so extensive a region as that of the free States could have been formed without some general council having been held, but it is true that there was no such council. These lines were formed in the following manner. There were anti-slavery men living at various points on the border of the free States. With them fugitives would stop, and this made it necessary for safety to find some anti-slavery men on the way, to whom these fugitives could be taken. I will give my own case as an instance. I lived on the top of a high hill at Ripley. My house was in full view of Kentucky. The slaves by some means discovered that I was an abolitionist, and consequently, when any of them ran away, they came to my house, and I knew that there were anti-slavery men on Red Oak, at Decatur, and Sardinia, and hence I could send them to any one of those places, and I had sons to convey them to such places as I chose to send them. And then they could be sent to Hillsborough, and then to Greenfield, and on from point to point until they arrived in Canada. In this way the various branches of the underground railway were formed. Could a history of the passengers on this road be written, it would be one of the most marvelous books the world has known. I will give some specimens of efforts made by slaves to gain freedom. A family of slaves lived near Dover, Ky. The mother of the family determined to free her husband and children. She commenced her enterprise by sending her husband to Canada. After he had entered into the land of liberty, she took her babe in her arms, and started for Canada. She designed to go to my house, but in mistake went to the house of a man who lived on a farm adjoining mine. In the night she knocked at the door; he opened it and saw her with her child in her arms; his compassion was deeply excited. He said to her 'Don't be afraid; I'm an abolitionist; but I have never come out yet. I'll help you.' He had hands working for him that he could not trust. He took her to a place of safety on the underground railway, and she went safely to Canada. She left six children in slavery. After four years she came back for her children on foot; for there were no back trains on the underground railway. She came to my house. She put on men's clothes, went over to Dover, and lay a whole day concealed in her master's garden, and held intercourse with four of her children. Two of her children were so young that she could not safely let them know of her being there, and they slept in the room in which the master and mistress slept; consequently she could not get them. During the night she started with four children and a grandchild, an infant; but failed to get over the river, and they were obliged to hide themselves in a field of green corn until the next night, and they had nothing but green corn to eat. The field was near Dover, and there was danger that the infant would cry so as to cause them to be discovered. A white man from Canada, who had fallen in with them, left them, and came over to Ohio. During the next night he went over after them and succeeded in getting them over the river to a house in Ripley, at which they had to spend a day. A daughter-in-law of the gentleman, at whose house they had taken refuge, rode in from the country with her babe in her lap. She left it, and took away the colored infant to her home in daylight. The slave-hunters were out, and in the town it was believed there were watchers. How to get the fugitives safely out of the place was a matter of consultation. There were some faithful young men in town who attended to cases of this kind. I advised them not to wait until they would be expected to go out; but in the dusk of the evening to pass them one at a time through a train of lots that extended across the town through which they could safely pass. In this way they passed on to my house, and then to another station, and safely on to Canada. Thus this brave woman freed her husband, herself, five children and a grandchild from slavery, and she had no white blood in her veins.

"At Augusta, Ky., there lived a pious black woman, a member of a Presbyterian Church, who was a slave. She had been brought up in a Presbyterian family, and was sold into a Methodist family in which she nursed the children. She was permitted to live some time as a free woman. Her master and mistress died, and she fell into the hands of the heirs, who determined to sell her. She was now fifty years of age. Such was her piety and good conduct that the better class of people at Augusta could not endure to have her sold, and hence some of them secreted her for some days. A colored girl, who lived in Ohio, went over at night and brought her away in a skiff to Ohio. She was brought to my house in the night. She had a mild and lovely countenance, as if illuminated with the rays of the Sun of righteousness. I was deeply moved in looking upon this daughter of the Almighty, secreted in my dwelling, and obliged, in old age, to travel hundreds of miles at night to escape from a land of horrible oppression. The Lord was with her, and she safely gained the land of liberty. It was a high privilege to be permitted to aid a child of God in such a time of distress. Seven valuable slaves started for Canada, and designed coming to my house but made the same mistake the colored woman made, and came at night to the house of my neighhor. He still had laborers, whom he felt that it was not safe to let know that he had fugitive slaves at his house. Consequently, he brought them to my house. After a little time he brought a large basket of provisions. He said if he could not keep them, he had a right to feed them. In the morning the slave-hunters came to town in pursuit. The fugitives saw their horses in the streets, and knew them. My neighbor went to town, and one of the slave-hunters having met him, said to him, 'I know it is not popular" in Ohio, for a gentleman to take up slaves, but if you will tell me where those slaves are, I will give you one thousand dollars and no one shall ever know it.' He could have pointed at my house, and said, they are in yonder house, and would have received one thousand dollars, and I would never have known that he did it. But he could not be bribed to do such a deed of wickedness. The fugitives were forwarded by night, to another State, and so on to Canada.

"A young man, a fugitive slave, came to my house. He said twenty men had been after him in a wheat field, and passed so near him that he feared they would hear his heart beat. He said the Kentuckians told him that the abolitionists of Ohio took off the runaway slaves and sold them; but said he, 'I was sold anyhow· and I thought I would try it.' He thought, if what they said was true, his case would be no worse than it was, as he was already sold to go South. When some young men came with horses to take him to another station, on bidding us farewell, he said, 'Oh, how good it is to find friends; can I not come back and see you all again?' No, I said, the laws are against you, and therefore you can not come back.

"A slave woman that lived opposite Ripley, was severely treated by her mistress, and consequently determined to leave for Canada. She took her infant in her arms and came to the house of a Scotchman, who lived on the bank of the river, and asked him to direct her what to do. He was an intemperate and wicked man, but he had not sinned away all his humanity. He said to her, 'A good man lives in that house on the hill beyond the river; cross over and go to that house; go right in, and you will be safe there. It was night; the river was frozen over; there came a thaw, and the river was about to break up; the water was running upon the ice ; she waded over, carrying her infant in her arms. She came to my house. The doors were not locked; she entered the kitchen, made a fire, dried her clothes, then searched for the family, found my sons, and asked them to help her. They arose and took her two miles further before day. Before morning the ice was broken up, and the river was impassable. Had she not dropped a piece of child's clothing on the Ohio side of the river, her pursuers would not have known but that she was drowned. She passed on to the neighborhood of Greenfield, and there she was obliged to remain until spring, in consequence of ice in the lakes.

„Within a few weeks afterward her

THE BATTLE.

husband left without leave to search for his wife and child. He went to the neighborhood of Greenfield. Some young men went to give notice that her husband had come. She became alarmed, thought they were Kentuckians come to take her back to slavery. She ran away with her child, and wandered about in the night until she and her child had almost perished with cold, and was forced to go to a house for shelter. A good Providence guided her to the house of a friend. When she met her husband she became so frantic that she could scarcely believe it was he. She shouted aloud, and manifested the most violent passion. Spring came, and they got safely to Canada.

"The master of a young man who had a wife and one child, determined to move from Kentucky to Missouri. He promised the young man that he would buy his wife and child, and take them with him. On these terms the young man was willing to go to Missouri. The master violated his promise, and determined to take the young man with him without his wife and child. When ready to start he ordered the young man to get his clothes and go with him. The young man went as if to get his clothes, and hid himself so that he could not be found; and after several days he went to Ohio, into a neighborhood of Quakers, a people who never turn the needy away from their doors unaided. In them he found true friends. His love for his wife and child was so ardent that he determined to have them at the risk of his liberty. A good Quaker brought him to Red Oak, five miles from the river. He came to my house, and by the help of a good man in Ripley he got his wife and two children safely to my house. One of them was born during his absence. He was exceedingly happy, and I and my family rejoiced with him. The good Quaker took him, with his wife and children, back to the Quaker neighborhood, and there was joy in that place. It was thought that they could dwell in perfect safety there, and hence they did not go on to Canada as they should have done. The hour of sorrow came. The young man went a hunting, and while he was absent a Methodist man came into the neighborhood pretending to buy hogs. He found the wife and children of this young man, and carried them off. The Quakers followed the villain, and overtook them at a village, but the villagers rose up to mob the Quakers and defend the man-stealer. The melancholy fact was published at Cincinnati in the *Philanthropist*. I read the article with the most painful sensations. My joy was turned into sorrow. The poor man lost his wife and children. He saw them no more.

"I will record another sad case : A fugitive returned to Kentucky to get his wife and two children. They were near Richmond, far distant from the Ohio River. He found his wife and children, and started for Canada. He was so closely pursued in Kentucky that he had to abandon one of his children. He succeeded in getting to Ripley. I then lived in town. He stopped with a colored man just across the street from my house. I knew nothing of his being there. The colored man undertook to convey him, with his wife and child, to the country. He met a slave-catcher who asked some questions, and galloped off to get help. The colored man became alarmed and hid them, and came back to town for help. The slave-catchers found them, pretended to be friends and took them off, put irons on the man and took him, his wife and child back to hopeless slavery. Poor man! Hope expired and all was lost. His long and hazardous journey to get his wife and children ended in the loss of himself.

THE BATTLE. 111

When I heard it I was seized with such anguish of spirit that it seemed as if there were nothing in creation that could cheer me. If he had been brought to my house he would have been safely conveyed to another depot and on to Canada. How near we may be to safety and yet lose all!

"The underground railway was kept in such good order that there was but little danger of miscarriage. Often whole families passed on safely to Canada. I have had under my roof as many as twelve fugitive slaves at a time, all of whom made good their way to Victoria's dominions. My house has been the door of freedom to many human beings, and while there was a hazard of life and property, there was much happiness in giving safety to the trembling fugitives. They were all children of God by creation, and some of them I believe were redeemed by the blood of the Lamb."

Yes, and if the children of God, no matter that their skins were black, or that they belonged to the lowly of earth, the Master will say for all such services, "Inasmuch as ye did unto one of the least of these my brethren, ye did it unto me." And knowing this fact, we can not but envy Mr. Rankin, that he was permitted to do so much work for the blessed Master.

CHAPTER V.

THE VICTORY.

WHATEVER may be the power of the Church in other lands we are not prepared to say, but in the United States her voice is potent, in the decision of all moral questions. Albert Barnes was right when he said that without the countenance of the Church slavery could not be sustained in the country a single day. George Junkin was right when he wrote that without the aid of the Thornwells and the Palmers of the Church, the South could never have succeeded in carrying the States into rebellion. This fact accounts for the determined effort made by the slave power to prevent the question being agitated in the Church. The cry of political preaching was raised, to which was added misrepresentation, disturbances of peace, etc.; that is, fire must be allowed to rage and consume the sleepers in the dwelling, because the cry necessary to arouse them might disturb some of their neighbors. Mr. Rankin, and many others, however, repudiated such logic, and raised their voices and sounded loud the alarm. "God will punish national sin by national judgments." It was believed by Mr. Rankin that this agitation had as much to do with the division of the Presbyterian Church as the question of doctrine; accordingly he, though Old School in his theology, cast in his lot with the New School branch, as its ministers and members were then considered far more anti-slavery than the other branch. But even in that branch the slaveholders were active and intolerant, and finally obtained temporary control in the Assembly; whereupon the Presbytery of Ripley, of which Mr. Rankin was a leading member refused to send delegates to its meetings. For this conduct the Presbytery was cited to appear before the Synod of Cincinnati with which it was connected. Mr. Rankin ably defended the Presbytery against the chief prosecutor, Mr. Hall, of Dayton, and the Presbytery was acquitted. The Rev. Mr. Graham replied to Mr. Rankin in a long speech, attempting to show that the Bible justified slaveholding. He afterward published it, and was suspended by Synod from the ministry for the sentiments it contained. The case was carried to the Assembly, and the proceedings of the Synod in the case condemned. In the meantime Ripley Presbytery, feeling greatly aggrieved by this action of the Assembly, issued a call for a convention to determine on the question of withdrawing from the jurisdiction of the Assembly. For this action they were censured at the subsequent meeting of

Synod, and without any previous consultation, one after another of the members of the Presbytery arose and asked to have their names stricken from the roll of Synod. The Convention referred to, had not yet met, and it is probable only for this action of Synod nothing would have been done at its meeting; but as it was, at its meeting after a sermon by Mr. Rankin, on the text, "Come out of her my people, that ye be not partakers of her sins," a new organization under the name of the "Free Presbyterian Church of America" was formed. From this body it was determined to exclude slaveholders and members of secret societies. A number of congregations from both branches of the Presbyterian Church soon joined this body, and a Synod was organized numbering some fifty ministers. What effect this new body had on the churches from which they had separated can not now be fully determined, but the anti-slavery

THE VICTORY. 117

cause prospered in both the bodies left, but more especially in the New School; so much so, that the Assembly that met in Detroit, in 1850, declared "Slavery a sin, and that it should be treated as other sins;" and the subsequent action of the Cleveland Assembly caused the slaveholding portion of the Assembly to secede. This opened up the way for the return of the Presbytery of Ripley to the Synod of Cincinnati.

During this same period the victory was being fought and won in the State. The principles which he had long inculcated, both by his voice and his pen, the principles which the Tract Society, which he was the instrument of organizing, had done so much to inculcate, were now becoming popular, and Abraham Lincoln, a representative of the anti-slavery idea, was elected President in the fall of 1860. The South seeing their power gone, and being assured that no longer in the North would the shout be heard, "Great is the Goddess Slavery," they raised the standard of rebellion, and determined to form a new nation with slavery as its corner stone, but God moved on the hearts of the people, and united them together in the determination to defend the life of the nation.

Defeat and discouragement, with here and there a victory to save us from despair, were given us by the God of battles until the nation was educated up to the point of accepting the help of the colored man, and then of proclaiming him free. And, just as we can not tell how much we are indebted to the sun, how much to the rain, the atmosphere and the soil, for the precious fruits of the earth, so we can not say how much any individual worker accomplished to gain this glorious victory. At the same time it is not too much to say that Rev. John Rankin, of Ripley, was one of the heroes in the conflict, one of the commanders that organized the victory. Often he had gone out bearing precious seed with tears; now with rejoicing he sees the sheaves gathered. During the earlier part of this period he experienced much trouble in his congregation, arising from causes not now worth naming, that resulted, finally, in a division of the congregation. Mr. Rankin went with the weaker part, and chiefly by his exertions a lot was obtained and a new house of worship erected. Both congregations continued to grow, but both felt that by their division their moral power was impaired, and finally they reunited, and called a new pastor, the infirmities of old age having admonished Mr. Rankin to resign, he having been pastor of the church for forty-four years.

The influence of Mr. Rankin was potent throughout and beyond the bounds of his own Synod, and we may add State;

for he not only frequently preached in various places and in the pulpits of several denominations, but he resorted to the Press to inculcate his views among his fellow-laborers, and his short pithy articles left impressions of truth in many hearts, though the subjects perhaps were not aware where or when they obtained them. He still lives at the age of seventy-five, and, like a victorious soldier as he is, he looks back with pleasure on the moral battles in which he has been engaged, and with much satisfaction he contemplates the fruits of the victories obtained. In a sense nearer that in which the Apostle spoke than most men can attain to, he will be able to say when the celestial messengers shall come to convey him home: "I have fought a good fight, I have kept the faith, henceforth there is laid up for me a crown of life."

www.ingramcontent.com/pod-product-compliance
Lightning Source LLC
Chambersburg PA
CBHW020129170426
43199CB00010B/703